better together*

* This book is best read together, grownup and kid.

 **akidsco.com**

a kids
book
about

a
kids
book
about
learning

by Kierra Shirley

A Kids Co.
Editor Emma Wolf
Designer Rick DeLucco
Creative Director Rick DeLucco
Studio Manager Kenya Feldes
Sales Director Melanie Wilkins
Head of Books Jennifer Goldstein
CEO and Founder Jelani Memory

DK
Delhi Technical Team Bimlesh Tiwary Pushpak Tyagi, Rakesh Kumar
Senior Production Editor Jennifer Murray
Senior Production Controller Louise Minihane
Senior Acquisitions Editor Katy Flint
Acquisitions Project Editor Sara Forster
Managing Art Editor Vicky Short
Managing Director, Licensing Mark Searle

First American edition, 2025
Published in the United States by DK Publishing, 1745 Broadway, 20th Floor,
New York, NY 10019

First published in Great Britain in 2025 by
Dorling Kindersley Limited, 20 Vauxhall Bridge Road, London SW1V 2SA
A Penguin Random House Company

The authorised representative in the EEA is
Dorling Kindersley Verlag GmbH. Arnulfstr. 124, 80636 Munich, Germany

A catalog record for this book is available from the Library of Congress.
A CIP catalogue record for this book is available from the British Library.
ISBN: 978-0-2417-4385-0

DK books are available at special discounts when purchased in bulk for sales
promotions, premiums, fund-raising, or education use. For details, contact:
DK Publishing Special Markets, 1745 Broadway, 20th Floor, New York, NY 10019
SpecialSales@dk.com

Printed and bound in China
www.dk.com
akidsco.com

MIX
Paper | Supporting
responsible forestry
FSC™ C018179

This book was made with Forest
Stewardship Council™ certified
paper – one small step in DK's
commitment to a sustainable future.
Learn more at www.dk.com/uk/
information/sustainability

To every child who has crossed my path
and the ones I hope to meet in the future:
I am honored to learn from you.

Intro
for grownups

What is the last thing you learned? Maybe a fun fact, a new skill, or someone's name?

A Kids Book About Learning explores the different ways people learn, and how we can find learning opportunities all around us. From babies learning the basics, to people understanding their best learning model, my hope is that your kid will see themself reflected in these pages.

Learning is not linear, and no one is great at learning *every* subject! Our strengths and difficulties are what make us human. Though sometimes it may feel challenging to be constantly learning, this book explores why it's important and ways to support and celebrate people who learn outside of what is considered "typical."

I hope this book provides you and your kid with a new lens on learning—and maybe even puts a pep in their step on their way to school!

Every brain is unique.

But **1** thing every brain does is................

..........learn.

I'm sure you're familiar with the word "learning," but do you know what it means?

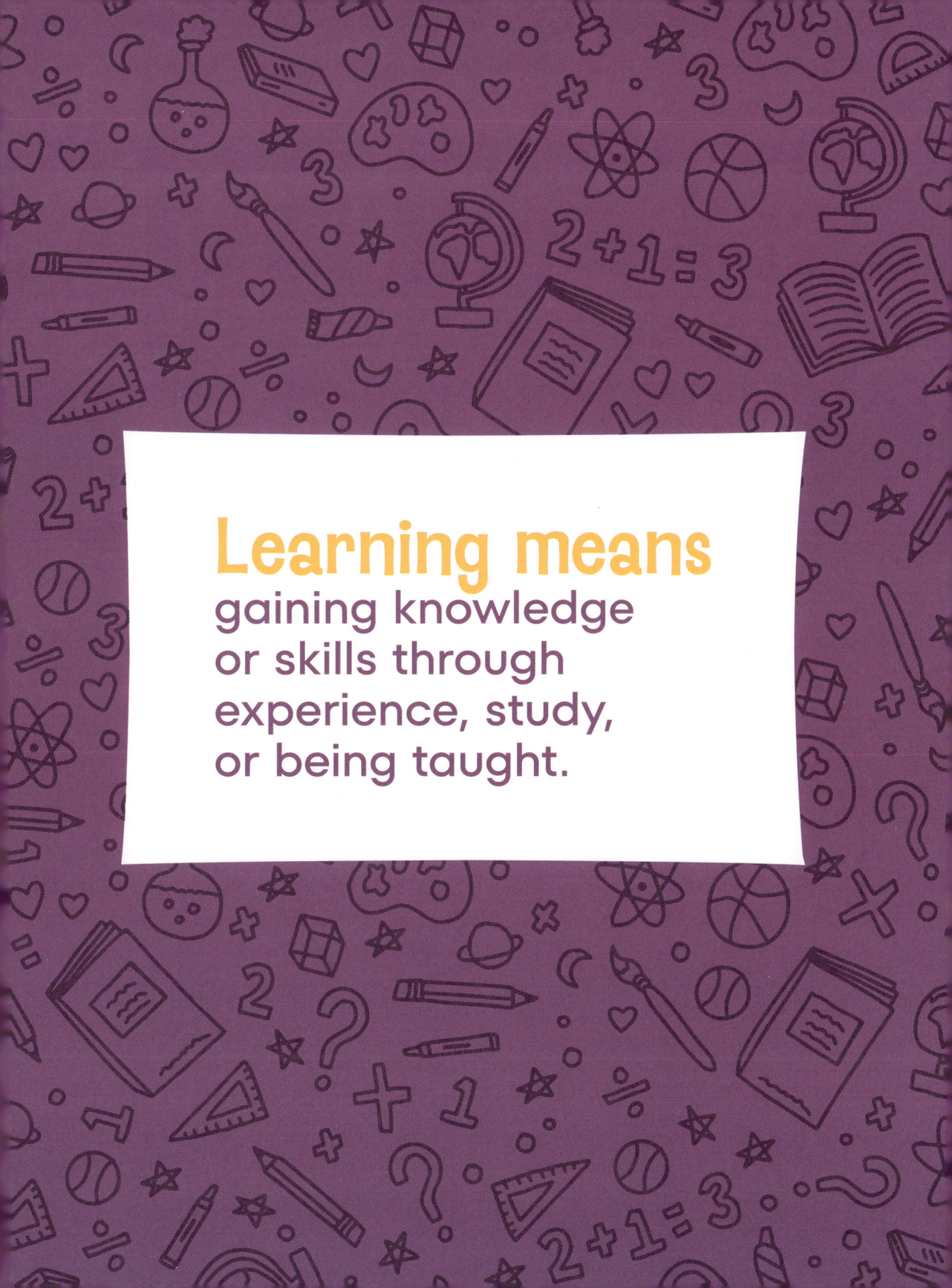

Learning means
gaining knowledge or skills through experience, study, or being taught.

So, what does *that* mean?

Let's start with babies.

They have a LOT of things to learn:

 **how to crawl,**

 **how to walk,**

 **how to talk,**

 **how to eat...**

♡ **how to *just be* a person!**

When you think about learning, is your first thought about school?

Have you ever thought about how much **YOU** learned before you even started school?

Humans are incredible!
AND THAT

MEANS YOU!

Learning can also look like...

playing a new instrument, joining a sports team, making a new friend, navigating life changes (like becoming a sibling!), traveling, trying new foods, making conversation with someone older than you, getting a new pet, visiting a museum, playing a computer game, celebrating different holidays, reading a new book, and lots of other things!

Learning happens all around you, all the time.

And learning isn't just for kids. NO WAY!

Ask your grownups or teachers. I promise, they're still learning every day, too!

No, seriously. Next time you're in class, ask your teacher what they're learning right now!

So, if we're all learning all the time...
it makes a lot of sense that we
would all learn differently.

Think about it.

I bet my life doesn't look exactly the same as yours, so we both have unique perspectives.

Everybody has things they're really good at, and everybody has areas where they can grow.

What are
some talents
you have?

What are some things you really love?

Whatever your

feel proud

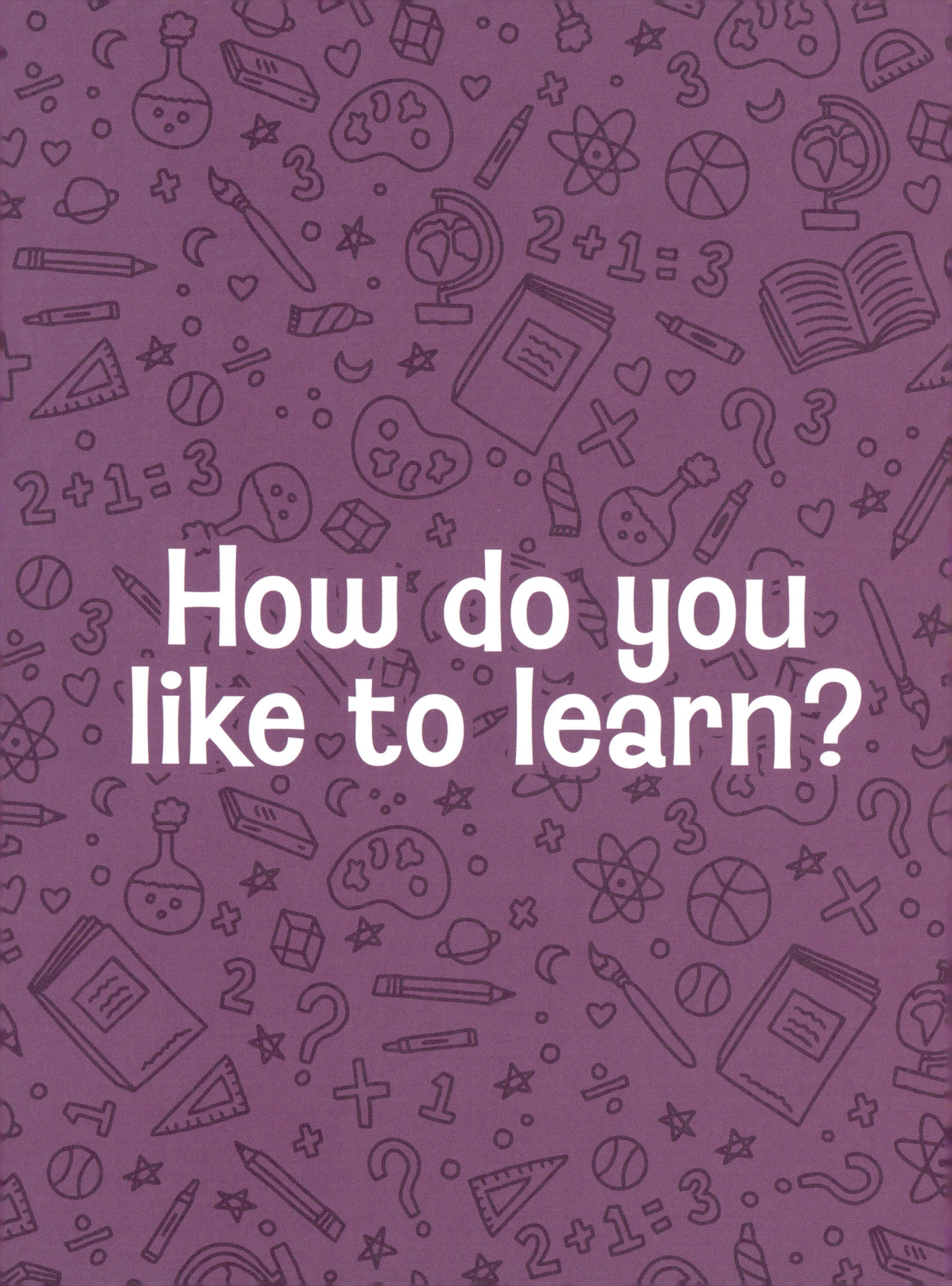

How do you like to learn?

strengths are,
of them.

Now, this might feel less fun, but...

what are some things you find challenging?

For me, spelling is really hard!

And maybe you're
great at spelling.

2+1=3.

The truth is,

it's a good thing that everyone has different areas they excel in.

The world is so much more
interesting because of it!

I have learned to understand kids' brains really well, and I use that skill in my job, every day. I love it!

I am a school psychologist, and I work to identify what might be causing kids to have difficulties learning.

Then, I work with their grownups and teachers to find ways we can help them succeed.

While everybody has natural differences in their learning, some people have what's called a

learning

disability.

A learning disability is a difference in someone's brain that makes it particularly hard to learn a specific kind of information.

Here are some of the most common learning disabilities I see.*

Dyslexia: when someone has a difference in the part of their brain that processes language. This makes things like reading and spelling difficult.

Dyscalculia: when someone has difficulty learning things which have to do with numbers.

Dysgraphia: when someone has difficulty with writing, either getting their thoughts on paper or writing legibly.

The very first thing I want you to know is that all brains are unique.

And because brains function differently, there are different ways people can learn and be taught.

Learning differences may be a challenge on your path to success.

That's OK!

All kids deserve to know how their brains work and why, so they can ask for what they need to best support their learning.

Have you really
thought about it before?

There are LOTS of ways to learn!

SMALL GROUPS
(BIG GROUPS CAN BE OVERWHELMING!)

INDEPENDENTLY

WITH HEADPHONES ON
(THE QUIET CAN BE HELPFUL)

THROUGH READING

THROUGH LISTENING

THROUGH WATCHING

IN A CHAIR THAT MOVES

BUILDING HANDS-ON PROJECTS

SPENDING TIME OUTSIDE

TAKING MOVEMENT BREAKS

WITH HELP FROM YOUR PEERS

WITH HELP FROM AN EXPERT
WITH SPECIAL
EDUCATION SERVICES
THROUGH TRYING
AND TRYING AGAIN
WITH ENCOURAGEMENT
USING THINGS YOU'VE
ALREADY LEARNED TO
APPROACH NEW CHALLENGES
LISTENING TO YOUR BODY AND WHAT
IT TELLS YOU IS NEEDED
BREAKING DOWN TASKS
INTO SMALL PARTS

Now that you know a little bit more,

is there a new learning technique you want to try?

With so many cool ways to learn, it's OK if you don't learn the same way as the person sitting next to you.

It's **OK** if how you learn changes over time.

It's OK if some days,
learning is just harder
than on other days.

Learning is a

lifelong journey.

So, you have the rest of your life to practice, figure out what works best for you, grow, and learn how you learn!

Learning is an adventure. Have

Outro
for grownups

You did it, you learned about learning! This book is a small part of a larger conversation about learning needs. While we touched on some factors which may impact learning, there are many others. It's important to consider the amount of exposure a kid has to given material, the quality and consistency of instruction, socioeconomic barriers, health, and safety (to name a few).

I hope that reading this book will spark conversations about your kid's unique brain and how they like to learn. I ask that you stay open to having conversations about your own learning strengths and challenges so your kids know that even their grownups are still learning!

Though not always easy, learning is what makes us who we are. Take some time to learn something new with your kiddo today!

If you are concerned about your kid's learning, please seek support from their school as well as their pediatrician.

About The Author

Kierra Shirley (she/her) wrote this book to celebrate different types of learners. As a school psychologist, she is a firm believer that ALL kids can learn. Through her work, she has seen a broad learning spectrum for kids with varying needs in an education system that does not always see them.

She hopes to set kids on this lifelong journey with confidence in and acceptance of themselves and others not *in spite of*, but *because of* their differences.

Everyone's learning journey is important regardless of the challenges they may face. Kierra hopes everyone can see themselves in this book and know that their brain is beautiful!

@kierra_shirley

Made to empower.

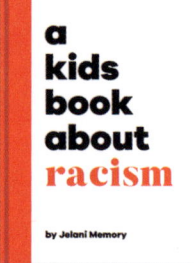    

    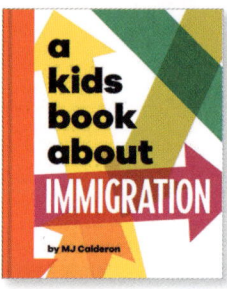

 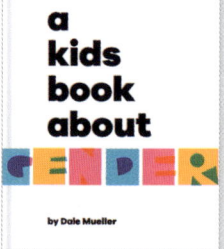 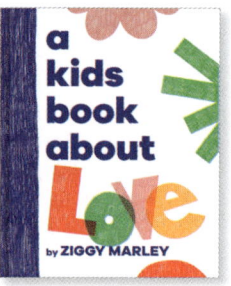  

  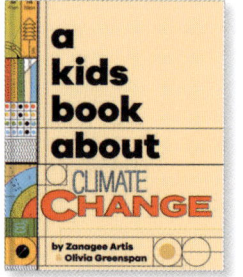  

Discover more at akidsco.com